Animal Kingdom Questions and Answers

Birds
A Question and Answer Book

by Isabel Martin

Consulting Editor: Gail Saunders-Smith, PhD

CAPSTONE PRESS
a capstone imprint

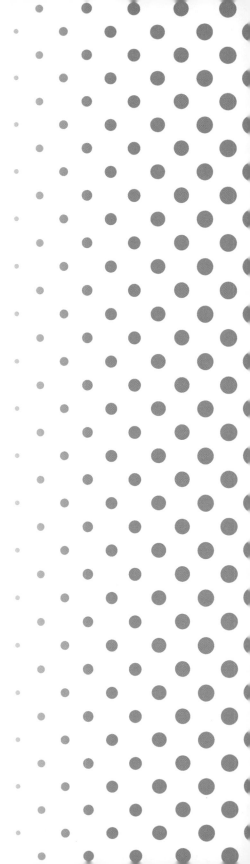

Pebble Plus is published by Capstone Press,
1710 Roe Crest Drive, North Mankato, Minnesota 56003
www.capstonepub.com

Library of Congress Cataloging-in-Publication Data
Martin, Isabel, 1977– author.
   Birds : a question and answer book / by Isabel Martin.
        pages cm. — (Pebble plus. Animal kingdom questions and answers)
   Summary: "Simple text and colorful images illustrate types of birds, including common characteristics, diet, and life cycle"—Provided by publisher.
   Audience: Ages 4–8.
   Audience: Grades K–3.
   Includes bibliographical references and index.
   ISBN 978-1-4914-0561-1 (library binding) — ISBN 978-1-4914-0629-8 (paperback) — ISBN 978-1-4914-0595-6 (eBook PDF)
   1. Birds—Miscellanea—Juvenile literature. 2. Children's questions and answers. I. Title.
   QL676.2.M3655 2015
   598.02—dc23   2013050345

Editorial Credits
Nikki Bruno Clapper, editor; Cynthia Akiyoshi, designer; Kelly Garvin, media researcher;
Katy LaVigne, production specialist

Photo Credits
Dreamstime/Charles Bruflag, cover, back cover; Shutterstock: BMJ, 9, BogdanBoev, 1, Cheryl E. Davis, 17, Emi, 15, jo Crebbin, 21, Karel Gallas, 19, Phillip Rubino, 5, Richard Susanto, 11, Sari ONeal, 7, Tero Hakala, 13

Note to Parents and Teachers

The Animal Kingdom Questions and Answers set supports national curriculum standards for science related to the diversity of living things. This book describes and illustrates the characteristics of birds. The images support early readers in understanding the text. The repetition of words and phrases helps early readers learn new words. This book also introduces early readers to subject-specific vocabulary words, which are defined in the Glossary section. Early readers may need assistance to read some words and to use the Table of Contents, Glossary, Read More, Internet Sites, Critical Thinking Using the Common Core, and Index sections of the book.

Printed in the United States of America in North Mankato, Minnesota.
032014   008087CGF14

Table of Contents

Meet the Birds

Whoosh! An eagle lands on a tree. Eagles, peacocks, and penguins are all birds. These animals come in many shapes, sizes, and colors.

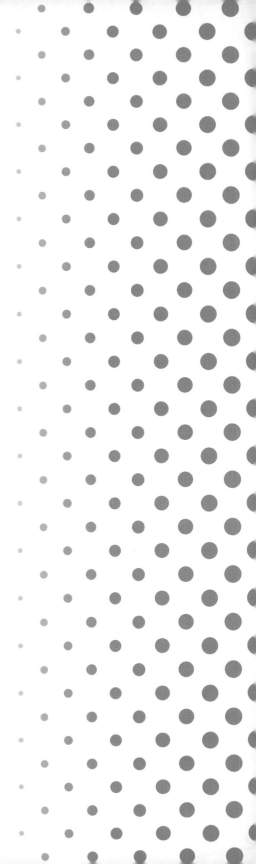

bald eagle

Do Birds Have Backbones?

Yes, birds have backbones.

Most birds have hollow areas

inside their bones.

Hollow bones help make

birds light so they can fly.

ruby-throated hummingbird

Are Birds Warm-Blooded or Cold-Blooded?

Birds are warm-blooded.

Their body temperature stays

the same in hot and cold weather.

emperor penguins

What Type of Body Covering Do Birds Have?

Birds have skin covered with feathers.

Most birds have scales on their feet.

All birds have wings and a bill.

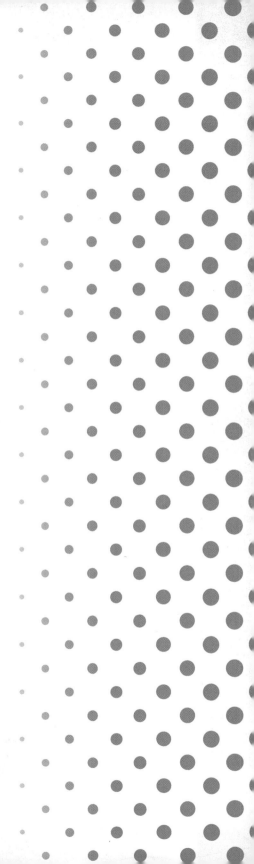

feathers

wing

bill

scales

African gray parrot

How Do Birds Eat?

Birds use their bills to eat.

Some birds eat seeds, fruit,

or worms. Other birds hunt

for fish, mice, snakes, or frogs.

osprey

Where Do Birds Live?

You can find birds almost anywhere.

Birds live in forests, deserts,

and even icy places. They also live

on beaches.

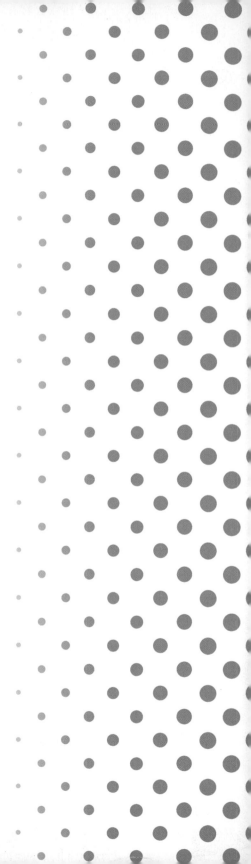

roadrunner

How Do Birds Have Young?

Birds lay eggs in a nest.

Then chicks hatch from the eggs.

Most chicks stay in the nest

until they can fly.

robins

Do Birds Care for Their Young?

Yes! Most birds sit on their eggs to keep them warm. They bring food to their chicks. Then they teach the chicks how to find food.

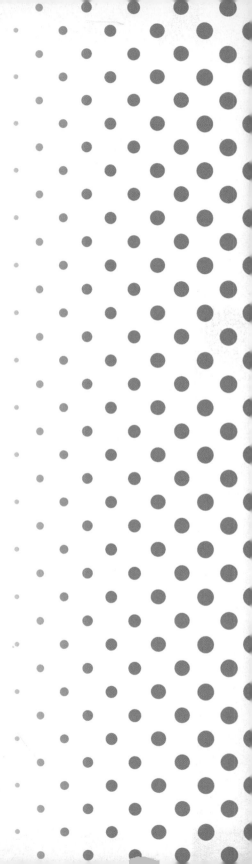

swans

What Is a Cool Fact About Birds?

Some birds cannot fly. Penguins waddle and swim instead of flying. Ostriches cannot fly either. But they can run very fast.

ostriches

Glossary

bill—the hard front part of the mouth of birds; also called a beak

chick—a young bird

hatch—to break out of an egg

hollow—empty on the inside

scale—a small, hard piece of skin that covers part or all of an animal's body

temperature—the measure of how hot or cold something is

warm-blooded—having a body temperature that stays about the same all the time

Read More

Bredeson, Carmen. *Weird Birds.* I Like Weird Animals! Berkeley Heights, N.J.: Enslow Publishers, Inc., 2010.

Schreiber, Anne. *Penguins!* National Geographic Science Readers. Washington, D.C.: National Geographic, 2009.

Sill, Cathryn. *About Birds: A Guide for Children.* Atlanta: Peachtree Publishers, 2014.

Internet Sites

FactHound offers a safe, fun way to find Internet sites related to this book. All of the sites on FactHound have been researched by our staff.

Here's all you do:
Visit www.facthound.com
Type in this code: 9781491405611

Check out projects, games and lots more at
www.capstonekids.com

Critical Thinking Using the Common Core

1. What body parts do all birds have? (Key Ideas and Details)

2. Look at the picture on page 17. What do these baby birds need? How do you think they will get what they need? (Integration of Knowledge and Ideas)

Index

Word Count: 190
Grade: 1
Early-Intervention Level: 16